ABOUT MAGIC READERS

ABDO continues its commitment to quality books with the nonfiction Magic Readers series. This series includes three levels of books to help students progress to being independent readers while learning factual information. Different levels are intended to reflect the stages of reading in the early grades, helping to select the best level for each individual student.

level 1

Level 1: Books with short sentences and familiar words or patterns to share with children who are beginning to understand how letters and sounds go together.

level 2

Level 2: Books with longer words and sentences and more complex language patterns with less repetition for progressing readers who are practicing common words and letter sounds.

level 3

Level 3: Books with more developed language and vocabulary for transitional readers who are using strategies to figure out unknown words and are ready to learn information more independently.

These nonfiction readers are aligned with the Common Core State Standards progression of literacy, following the sequence of skills and increasing the difficulty of language while engaging the curious minds of young children. These books also reflect the increasing importance of reading informational material in the early grades. They encourage children to read for fun and to learn!

Hannah E. Tolles, MA Reading Specialist

www.abdopublishing.com

Published by Magic Wagon, a division of ABDO, PO Box 398166, Minneapolis, Minnesota 55439. Copyright © 2015 by Abdo Consulting Group, Inc. International copyrights reserved in all countries. No part of this book may be reproduced in any form without written permission from the publisher. Magic Readers™ is a trademark and logo of Magic Wagon.

Printed in the United States of America, North Mankato, Minnesota.
042014
092014

Cover Photo: Thinkstock
Interior Photos: Glow Images, iStockphoto, Thinkstock

Written and edited by Rochelle Baltzer, Heidi M. D. Elston,
    Megan M. Gunderson, and Bridget O'Brien
Illustrated by Candice Keimig
Designed by Candice Keimig and Jillian O'Brien

Library of Congress Cataloging-in-Publication Data

Baltzer, Rochelle, 1982- author.
  Dolphins in the ocean / written and edited by Rochelle Baltzer
[and three others] ; designed and illustrated by Candice Keimig.
    pages cm. -- (Magic readers, level 3)
  Audience: Ages 5-8.
  ISBN 978-1-62402-068-1
1. Dolphins--Juvenile literature. I. Keimig, Candice,
illustrator. II. Title.
  QL737.C432B367 2015
  599.53--dc23
            2014001070

Magic Readers

level 3

Dolphins
in the Ocean

By Rochelle Baltzer
Illustrated photos by Candice Keimig

Magic Readers

An Imprint of Magic Wagon
www.abdopublishing.com

Bottlenose dolphins live in oceans around the world.

They prefer warm water. So, they do not live in very cold water.

Some dolphins live offshore in deep water.

Others live near coasts and swim into bays.

Dolphins share their ocean home
with many other animals.

Sharks, turtles, jellyfish, fish, and clams are some of them.

Shark

Turtle

Jellyfish

Fish

Clam

Dolphins watch out for predators in the ocean.

Killer whales and great white
sharks eat dolphins.

Dolphins swim through the ocean in groups, or pods.

The largest dolphin in the pod is the leader.

Pods sometimes join to make herds.

There can be hundreds of dolphins in a herd!

Some dolphins move to warmer water during cold seasons.

This is called migrating. One reason animals migrate is to find food.

Dolphins find all the food they
need in the ocean.

They eat almost any kind of fish.
They also eat squid and shrimp.

Dolphins like to follow fishing boats.

They hope to eat some leftover
fish!

Sometimes, oceans become dirty.
This can make dolphins sick.

People work to protect the oceans.
They want dolphins to be healthy.

People enjoy spotting dolphins in the ocean. They see their fins pop up as they are swimming!